BELGICA

GAULISH VILLAGE

COMPENDIUM

LAUDANUM

AQUARIUM

TOTORUM

ARMORICA

LUTETIA

SPQR

GAUL
(ROMAN CONQUEST)
50 BC

CELTICA

AQUITANIA

PROVINCIA

THE YEAR IS 50 BC. GAUL IS ENTIRELY OCCUPIED BY THE ROMANS. WELL, NOT ENTIRELY . . . ONE SMALL VILLAGE OF THE INDOMITABLE GAULS STILL HOLDS OUT AGAINST THE INVADERS. AND LIFE IS NOT EASY FOR THE ROMAN LEGIONARIES WHO GARRISON THE FORTIFIED CAMPS OF TOTORUM, AQUARIUM, LAUDANUM AND COMPENDIUM . . .

ASTERIX, THE HERO OF THESE ADVENTURES. A SHREWD, CUNNING LITTLE WARRIOR, ALL PERILOUS MISSIONS ARE IMMEDIATELY ENTRUSTED TO HIM. ASTERIX GETS HIS SUPERHUMAN STRENGTH FROM THE MAGIC POTION BREWED BY THE DRUID GETAFIX . . .

OBELIX, ASTERIX'S INSEPARABLE FRIEND. A MENHIR DELIVERY-MAN BY TRADE, ADDICTED TO WILD BOAR. OBELIX IS ALWAYS READY TO DROP EVERYTHING AND GO OFF ON A NEW ADVENTURE WITH ASTERIX – SO LONG AS THERE'S WILD BOAR TO EAT, AND PLENTY OF FIGHTING. HIS CONSTANT COMPANION IS DOGMATIX, THE ONLY KNOWN CANINE ECOLOGIST, WHO HOWLS WITH DESPAIR WHEN A TREE IS CUT DOWN.

GETAFIX, THE VENERABLE VILLAGE DRUID, GATHERS MISTLETOE AND BREWS MAGIC POTIONS. HIS SPECIALITY IS THE POTION WHICH GIVES THE DRINKER SUPERHUMAN STRENGTH. BUT GETAFIX ALSO HAS OTHER RECIPES UP HIS SLEEVE . . .

CACOFONIX, THE BARD. OPINION IS DIVIDED AS TO HIS MUSICAL GIFTS. CACOFONIX THINKS HE'S A GENIUS. EVERYONE ELSE THINKS HE'S UNSPEAKABLE. BUT SO LONG AS HE DOESN'T SPEAK, LET ALONE SING, EVERYBODY LIKES HIM . . .

FINALLY, VITALSTATISTIX, THE CHIEF OF THE TRIBE. MAJESTIC, BRAVE AND HOT-TEMPERED, THE OLD WARRIOR IS RESPECTED BY HIS MEN AND FEARED BY HIS ENEMIES. VITALSTATISTIX HIMSELF HAS ONLY ONE FEAR, HE IS AFRAID THE SKY MAY FALL ON HIS HEAD TOMORROW. BUT AS HE ALWAYS SAYS, TOMORROW NEVER COMES.

Asterix titles available now

Original edition © 1983 Les Éditions Albert René / Goscinny-Uderzo
English translation © 1983 Les Éditions Albert René / Goscinny-Uderzo
Original title: *Le Fils d'Astérix*

Exclusive licensee: Orion Publishing Group
Translators: Anthea Bell and Derek Hockridge
Typography: Bryony Newhouse

This revised edition first published in 2001 by Orion Books Ltd,
Orion House, 5 Upper Saint Martin's Lane, London WC2H 9EA
An Hachette UK company

7 9 10 8

Printed in China

www.asterix.com
www.orionbooks.co.uk

A CIP record for this book is available from the British Library

ISBN 978-0-7528-4714-6 (cased)
ISBN 978-0-7528-4775-7 (paperback)

The Orion Publishing Group's policy is to use papers that are natural, renewable and recyclable products
and made from wood grown in sustainable forests. The logging and manufacturing processes are
expected to conform to the environmental regulations of the country of origin.

THE SUN IS RISING OVER ASTERIX'S VILLAGE, AS USUAL. THE SCENE IS ONE OF PEACE AND SERENITY...

...DISTURBED, DESPITE THE FACT THAT DAY IS DAWNING BY THE SNORES OF THE ONLY GAULISH ROOSTER WHO HAS ADENOIDS.

SNORT! ZZZ!

IT'S COCKCROW, YOU GOOSE! TIME TO TALK TURKEY.

YOU'RE IN A FOWL MOOD THIS MORNING!

TAP! TAP! TAP!

COCK-A-DOODLE-DOO

YAWN!

COME ON, GET UP! IT'S GOING TO BE A LOVELY DAY!

I HAD SUCH A FUNNY DREAM LAST NIGHT, ASTERIX!

SCRATCH! SCRATCH!

I DREAMED THE STORKS VISITED OUR VILLAGE, BRINGING THE BABIES PEOPLE HAD ORDERED, AND ONE OF THEM LEFT A BABY HERE BY MISTAKE!

SCRATCH! SCRATCH!

DON'T SAY YOU STILL BELIEVE STORKS DELIVER BABIES!

WHY NOT? I DELIVER MENHIRS, DON'T I?

ONE OF THESE DAYS YOU AND I MUST HAVE A LITTLE TALK, OBELIX!

CREEAK!

GA! GA!

?

GOO! GOO!

GURGLE!

I SEE YOUR PROBLEM, ASTERIX! WE MUST FIND OUT WHERE THE BABY COMES FROM AND WHOSE HE IS. IT'S URGENT!

I MUST JUST POINT OUT THAT FOUNDLINGS ARE USUALLY DUMPED ON TEMPLE DOORSTEPS OR IN PUBLIC PLACES...

...SO THAT WHEN A BABY IS RATHER POINTEDLY LEFT OUTSIDE A BACHELOR WARRIOR'S HUT, PEOPLE ARE BOUND TO THINK THINGS!

THINGS? WHAT THINGS?

4A

HEY! HANG ON! ARE YOU OUT OF YOUR MINDS?

TAP! TAP! TAP!

ONE MIGHT EVEN THINK MISTER ASTERIX WOULD HAVE NO TROUBLE IN FINDING THAT BABY'S MOTHER!

YOU DON'T MINCE YOUR WORDS, DO YOU? SHUT UP, OR I'LL MAKE MINCEMEAT OF **YOU!**

CALM DOWN! WE MUSTN'T GET UPSET!

ASTERIX! COME QUICK!!!

THAT'S OBELIX CALLING ME!!!

ASTERIiiiiiX!

MOOOOOOOO!

DING! DING! DING!

AND IT LOOKED LIKE BEING SUCH A LOVELY DAY!

4B

DING DING DING DING

DING DING DING!

MOOOOOOOO!

GOO, GOO!

HE TAKES BUCOLIX'S COW FOR A RATTLE, ASTERIX!

?

BY TOUTATIS, I BET YOU WENT AND MADE HIS BOTTLE OUT OF A GOURD WHICH WAS STILL HALF FULL OF **MAGIC POTION!**

WON'T IT BE BAD FOR HIM, GETAFIX?

DON'T WORRY! OBELIX IS LIVING PROOF OF THE FACT MAGIC POTION IS HARMLESS TO BABIES...

GA!

SPLATCH!

GEDOING!

THOUGH MAYBE NOT TO THOSE IN THEIR VICINITY!

5a

GOTTA LOTTA BOTTLE, EH? YOU WANT A SMACKED BOTTOM!

GA?

GNNNNNNNNN!

GOO! GA! TEEHEE!

HMPH!

BLAMM!

I DON'T KNOW WHAT BABIES ARE COMING TO THESE DAYS, ASTERIX!

HERE'S YOUR COW... A BIT RATTLED, BUT OK!

?!

AND NEXT TIME SHE SEES A BABY, MIND SHE DOESN'T LOOK SO LIKE A TOY! RATTLING COWS IS BAD FOR THEM!

??? ??? ? ?

5b

CHIEF VITALSTATISTIX, WHAT AM I GOING TO DO ABOUT THIS BABY?

CLUCK!

DON'T YOU THINK YOU'VE DONE ENOUGH ALREADY?

AND DON'T TOUCH THAT CHILD WITH YOUR CLUMSY GREAT HANDS! WHAT HE NEEDS IS A MOTHER'S TENDER CARE!

DON'T YOU, MY LITTLE SWEETIE-PIE?

GA?

POC!

?

YOU COME HOME WITH ME!

AND IN FUTURE, I DON'T WANT YOU MIXING WITH PEOPLE WHOSE EFFECT ON ALL AROUND THEM IS SO DEVASTATING!

BUT IMPEDIMENTA, DEAR...

?

CLUCK!

I THINK THIS BABY HAS HIS HEAD SCREWED ON THE RIGHT WAY!

GA!

WELL, THAT SETTLES IT, ASTERIX!

HE'S DEFINITELY PICKED YOU TWO FOR HIS ADOPTIVE FATHERS!

ASTERIX AND OBELIX, THE GUARDIANSHIP OF THIS CHILD, WITH ALL ITS WEIGHTY RESPONSIBILITIES, IS NOW YOURS. TAKE GOOD CARE OF HIM!

I WILL NOW GIVE YOU AN ODE ON THE JOYS OF FAMILY LIFE!

YOU TRY IT!

HE'S GONE TO SLEEP! NO BIGGER THAN A WILD BOAR PIGLET, AND HE'S AS MUCH TROUBLE AS MAKING FIFTY MENHIRS!

WHO ON EARTH CAN HAVE BEEN BOLD ENOUGH TO ABANDON THIS BABY?

I TOLD YOU. IT MUST HAVE BEEN A STORK WHO...

SHUT UP ABOUT STORKS, OR I SHALL DO YOU AN INJURY!

SSSH! YOU'LL WAKE HIM UP, AND THEN HE'LL WANT A COW TO RATTLE!

THAT'S WHAT COMES OF BEING FOOL ENOUGH TO GIVE HIM A BOTTLE OF MILK WITH MAGIC POTION IN IT!

HARK AT MISTER ASTERIX! FULL OF THE MILK OF HUMAN KINDNESS, AREN'T YOU? WHO'S A MILKSOP, THEN?

MILKSOP YOURSELF! IT'S YOUR SOPPY FAULT!

OH, REALLY? YOU DON'T BELIEVE IN BOTTLING UP A GRIEVANCE DO YOU?

YOU'RE ENOUGH TO MAKE ME TAKE TO THE BOTTLE MYSELF!

WAAAAA!

!

7A

WAAAA!!

THERE! WHAT DID I TELL YOU?

I THINK IT'S HIGH TIME WE WENT IN SEARCH OF THAT BABY'S PARENTS!

SO A LITTLE LATER...

ASTERIX, HOW ARE WE GOING TO RECOGNIZE PARENTS WHO WON'T EVEN RECOGNIZE THEIR OWN CHILD?

WE DO HAVE ONE CLUE: THE BABY'S CLOTHES AND WRAPPINGS ARE MADE OF EMBROIDERED LINEN, THE SORT OF THING YOU'D EXPECT TO FIND IN A RICH ROMAN FAMILY...

SO WE'LL START BY INVESTIGATING THE FORTIFIED ROMAN CAMPS THAT SURROUND THE VILLAGE!

OH, GOODY! I LOVE INVESTIGATING ROMAN CAMPS!

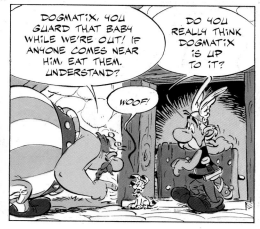

DOGMATIX, YOU GUARD THAT BABY WHILE WE'RE OUT! IF ANYONE COMES NEAR HIM, EAT THEM. UNDERSTAND?

WOOF!

DO YOU REALLY THINK DOGMATIX IS UP TO IT?

OF COURSE! HE'S HAD LOTS OF EXPERIENCE. I'VE TAUGHT HIM TO GUARD MENHIRS!

!!!

7B

?!

AVE, GAULS!

I AM CRISMUS CACTUS, PREFECT OF GAUL, AND I HAVE COME TO INVESTIGATE THE WHOLE OF THIS CONQUERED TERRITORY AND TAKE A CENSUS OF THE GAULISH VILLAGES!

YOU'VE GOT ONE THING WRONG, ROMAN! THIS VILLAGE STILL HOLDS OUT AGAINST THE INVADERS!

AND WE'RE THE ONES DOING THE INVESTIGATING!

WE'LL SEE ABOUT THAT! **READY MEN? AT THE WORD...**

THIS IS A GREAT START TO OUR INVESTIGATIONS, ASTERIX...

GLUG! GLUG! GLUG!

8A

PATCHAC!

SIGNA INFERRE! PRAEGE! CONCURSU! AD GLADIOS! INFESTIS PILIS!*

* FORWARD! MARCH! CHARGE! TO ARMS! TAKE AIM!

DISMOUNT!

BONK!

SINCE WE'RE MAKING INVESTIGATIONS, DO YOU HAPPEN TO KNOW OF ANY ROMANS WHO ABANDONED THEIR BABY OUTSIDE ASTERIX'S HUT?

!!!

DON'T BOTHER OBELIX. ANYONE CAN SEE THEY'RE NEW TO THESE PARTS! LETS GO TO COMPENDIUM!

WELL, NOW I KNOW ENOUGH TO GO BACK TO CONDATUM.*

8B

* RENNES

WELL, NOW FOR AQUARIUM, THE LAST FORTIFIED ROMAN CAMP!

SOON AFTERWARDS...

WE'RE TRYING TO FIND OUT WHO ABANDONED THIS BABY AND MAKING SOME INVESTIGATIONS!

YOUR METHODS ARE CERTAINLY STRIKING!

I KNOW SOMEONE WHO MAY BE ABLE TO HELP YOU!

WE HAD A VISIT FROM A PREFECT THIS MORNING. HE'S GOING AROUND TAKING A CENSUS OF ALL THE LOCAL GAULS!

WE KNOW THAT! SO?

SO THAT'S JUST A PRETEXT! THE PREFECT TOLD ME HIS REAL JOB WAS TO LOOK FOR A BABY. IT MIGHT WELL BE THIS ONE!

QUICK, OBELIX! WE MUST FIND THAT PREFECT AGAIN!

ROMAN CAMPS ARE LIKE POCKETS... YOU NEVER FIND WHAT YOU'RE AFTER TILL YOU GET TO THE LAST ONE!

IF SO MANY RESOURCES ARE BEING DEPLOYED TO FIND HIM, THAT BABY MUST BELONG TO A POWERFUL FAMILY!

THAT'S WHAT MAKES HIM SO STRONG! NOTHING TO DO WITH THE POTION, EH, MY BOY?

GA!

CAREFUL! I HEAR VOICES!!!

AND THE PREFECT SAID NOT TO WORRY, TAKING A CENSUS IS DEAD EASY, HE SAID! EASY AND SAFE... ALL YOU HAVE TO KNOW IS HOW TO COUNT, HE SAID!

YEAH... COUNT YOUR BRUISES!

WELL HE CAN'T COUNT ON ME ANY MORE!

QUOD ERAT DEMONSTRANDUM!

SHUT UP AND KEEP LIMPING!

THE GAULS!

CALM DOWN, ROMANS! JUST TAKE US TO YOUR LEADER, PREFECT CACTUS! WE WANT TO TALK TO HIM!

STAY HERE AND BE GOOD, OKAY?

GA?

GRRRR

HE CAST US ASIDE LIKE AN OLD DIGITABULUM* AND HE WENT OFF TO CONDATUM IN A HURRY!

* ROMAN GLOVE

OHO! THIS MUST BE THE BABY CRISMUS CACTUS IS, LIKE, YKNOW, LOOKING FOR! IF I TAKE HIM THE CHILD HE'LL MAKE ME SORT OF, OPTIO, YKNOW, AND COVER ME, LIKE, WITH GOLD!

SO WHO'S COUNTING ON THE RESULTS OF THIS CENSUS?

NOT CAESAR, ANYWAY. HE'S BUSY WITH THE TROUBLES IN UPPER GERMANIA!

I'LL SEIZE MY CHANCE WHILE THEY'RE ALL, LIKE, TALKING! TEEHEE!

HELP! HELP!

?

12A

OH, LOOK, HE WANTS TO RATTLE A ROMAN NOW!

HEEEELLLLLLP!

PAF!

GOO! GOO!

YOU KNOW, WE TWO HAVE A LOT IN COMMON!

GA!

RUN FOR IT! BIG GAULS HAVE LITTLE GAULS UPON THEIR BACKS TO BITE 'EM...

OR US! AND LITTLE GAULS HAVE LESSER GAULS...

AND SO AD INFINITUM!

SHUT UP AND KEEP GOING!

12B

MEANWHILE, AT CONDATUM, IN THE RESIDENCE OF THE PREFECT OF ARMORICA...

QUICK! SEND A MESSENGER OFF TO ROME!

DON'T BOTHER, CACTUS!

BRUTUS!?

THAT'S RIGHT! I'VE COME FROM ROME SPECIALLY TO HEAR THE LATEST ABOUT OUR LITTLE AFFAIR!

JUDGING BY YOUR SLOVENLY APPEARANCE, CONTACT WITH THE LOCAL BARBARIANS IS BAD FOR YOU!

CONTACT WITH THEIR FISTS IS! THIS INVESTIGATION YOU WANTED MADE IS A RISKY BUSINESS!

HAVE YOU FOUND THE BABY?

YES, I HAVE. HE'S IN A LITTLE VILLAGE ON THE NORTH COAST... BUT GUARDED BY TWO FIERCE GAULS WHO FLATTENED AN ENTIRE INFANTRY SECTION!

HMM... CAESAR'S OFTEN TOLD ME ABOUT THAT VILLAGE OF CRAZY BUT INDOMITABLE GAULS WHO GET THEIR STRENGTH FROM DRINKING MAGIC POTION!

13A

BUT I'LL HAVE THAT BABY EVEN IF I HAVE TO PUT ALL GAUL TO FIRE AND THE SWORD!!!

LUCKILY, SOME WAY OFF...

COME ON, SON, TRY YOUR LEGS OUT!

GA!

LOOK, ASTERIX! HE KNOWS HIS HOME ALREADY!

?!

BANG!

?!

JUST LIKE ME AT HIS AGE!

I WONDER IF WE'RE SETTING THAT CHILD A GOOD EXAMPLE?

AGA!

13B

17

LATER...

WELL, THE DOOR'S REPAIRED, THE BABY'S ASLEEP AND DOGMATIX IS ON GUARD. SO LET'S GO AND DISCUSS THE SITUATION WITH CHIEF VITALSTATISTIX!

I'VE GOT TO DELIVER A MENHIR TO BUCOLIX FIRST!

MENHIRS HAVE A LONG SHELF LIFE... CAN'T IT WAIT?

NO, IT CAN'T. I ALWAYS MAKE SURE MY MENHIRS ARE SHIFTED BEFORE THE 'SELL BY' DATE!

SO THE ROMANS KNOW THE BABY IS HERE, AND THIS FAKE CENSUS OF THEIRS SUGGESTS THAT THEIR INTENTIONS AREN'T ENTIRELY HONOURABLE!

BUT WE STILL DON'T KNOW WHY SOMEONE CHOSE OUR VILLAGE AS THE PLACE TO LEAVE THE BABY.

I THINK I KNOW WHY!

THE BABY MUST NEED PROTECTION FROM THE ROMANS... AND OUR VILLAGE IS THE ONE SAFE PLACE WHERE ROMANS WOULD NEVER DARE TO COME!

CRAAASH! ? ?

ASTERIX, SINCE I'M GOING TO SEE BUCOLIX ANYWAY, WOULD YOU LIKE ME TO PICK UP ANOTHER COW FOR THE LITTLE LAD?

OBELIX, MY BOY, I WISH TO GOODNESS YOU'D TAKE YOUR MENHIR OFF WHEN YOU COME INDOORS!

BUT, CHIEF, MENHIRS ARE HIGH FASHION INDOORS AS WELL AS OUT!

TOO HIGH FOR MY DOOR BY HALF, YOU IDIOT!

HE GETS FUNNY MOODS, DOES VITAL-STATISTIX! IT'S NOT MY FAULT IF HIS DOOR ISN'T UP TO MY MENHIRS!

I'VE BROUGHT YOU THIS MENHIR TO PAY FOR THE HIRE OF YOUR COW, BUCOLIX!

OH, ARR! THERE BE SUMMAT OI WANTS TO ASK YOU, OBELIX... WHAT WERE YOU A-DOIN' OF WITH SHE? SHE BE PROPER COWED! SHE'VE NOBBUT TO SEE A BABBY NOW AND SHE DO BE CLIMBIN' TREES!

LOOK, HOW ABOUT A REGULAR MILK RUN? YOU DELIVER MILK BY THE BUCKET, UNPACKAGED, SAME AS I DELIVER MENHIRS! WHERE SHALL I PUT THIS ONE?

OI'LL 'AVE IT IN THAT THERE FIELD, ALONG OF T'OTHERS!

ISN'T THAT BEAUTIFUL! ER... WHAT DO YOU USE YOUR MENHIR COLLECTION FOR?

OI DON'T USE THAT FOR NOWT... THEY DO SAY AS THE LAND HEREABOUTS BAIN'T NO GOOD FOR GROWIN' NOWT BUT STONES, SO OI MOIGHT AS WELL SEE IF THAT BE AN OLD WOIVES' TALE!*

*A SIMILAR EXPERIMENT WAS THEN GOING ON AT STONEHENGE.

15ᵃ

SOON AFTER...

I THINK IT MIGHT BE WISER FOR ONE OF US TO STAY AT HOME AND BABYSIT WHEN WE HAVE TO GO OUT IN FUTURE, OBELIX!

OH YES? WHICH ONE?

WELL, IN A WORD, YOU!

WORDS FAIL ME! WHY NOT YOU?

BECAUSE MY TACT AND DELICACY ARE BETTER THAN YOURS WHEN IT COMES TO LOOKING FOR THAT BABY'S PARENTS, AND THAT'S MY LAST WORD!

OH, MY WORD!??!!

15ᵇ

19

BUT IN CONDATUM...

SO NOW YOU KNOW THE DREADFUL SECRET OF THAT CHILD'S BIRTH, CACTUS!

AND YOU ALSO KNOW THE EQUALLY DREADFUL SECRET OF MY PLAN! IF YOU BETRAY ME, IT WILL BE THE WORSE FOR YOU!

WHAT, ME, BETRAY YOU? DO I LOOK LIKE A TRAITOR?

YES! BUT I HAVE NO CHOICE. SO IF YOU SERVE ME WELL, YOU'LL GET THAT SEAT IN THE ROMAN SENATE YOU'VE BEEN WANTING SO LONG!

I'D SELL MY MOTHER AND FATHER TO SERVE YOU IF I HADN'T DONE THAT ALREADY, O BRUTUS, SON OF CAESAR!

ONLY ADOPTED SON OF CAESAR, AND ALL I'M ASKING YOU TO DO IS BRING ME THAT BABY!

I HAVE AN IDEA!

FLOP!

WAAAAH!

ASTERIX, SUPPOSE I GAVE HIM JUST ONE TINY DROP OF MAGIC POTION, MAYBE HE'D...

YOU'LL DO NO SUCH THING! YOU TWO HAVE CREATED ENOUGH HAVOC ALREADY!!!

ALL RIGHT, ALL RIGHT, I GET THE IDEA! MUSTN'T TREAT THIS PLACE LIKE HOME, MUST WE, DOGMATIX?

WAAAAH!

WAAAAH!

HEY... HE'S LEFT ME HOLDING THE BABY! OH, VERY CLEVER, MISTER OBELIX!

21

O DRUID, WE MUST DO SOMETHING! WE'RE GAULISH WARRIORS... WE'VE NO IDEA HOW TO BRING UP A BABY!

THE TROUBLE IS, YOU AND OBELIX ARE THE ONLY PEOPLE HE'LL HAVE NEAR HIM!

BUT NOW THE EFFECTS OF THE MAGIC POTION HAVE WORN OFF, MAYBE WE COULD HAND HIM OVER TO A NURSEMAID?

IT'S WORTH A TRY!

ANYWAY, HE'S STOPPED CRYING! THE WORST IS OVER!

OR YET TO COME! I HAVE A NASTY KIND OF FEELING...

OH, BY TOUTATIS, I THOUGHT SO! HE'S GONE AGAIN!

19 A

HE MIGHT GET INTO TROUBLE... WE MUST FIND HIM!

WE ONLY HAVE TO FOLLOW DOGMATIX!

LUCKILY DOGMATIX IS BRIGHTER THAN THOSE STORKS!

SNIFF! SNIFF!

IT LOOKS AS IF THE BABY'S IN YOUR HOUSE, GETAFIX!

SNIFF! SNIFF!

ASTERIX! THE BABY'S FALLEN INTO THE CAULDRON OF MAGIC POTION!

OH NO! THAT REMINDS ME OF SOMETHING..!

WOOF! WOOF!

THERE WASN'T MUCH POTION LEFT... BUT ENOUGH FOR THE EFFECTS TO LAST LONGER THIS TIME!

YOU KNOW, I REALLY TAKE TO YOU!

BURP!

AND TO THINK I ONLY FEARED THE WORST!

19 B

MEANWHILE, NOT FAR FROM THE VILLAGE...

O MARCUS JUNIUS BRUTUS, SINCE WE WANT OUR HQ NEAR THE INDOMITABLE GAULS, WHY DON'T WE USE ONE OF THE FORTIFIED CAMPS SURROUNDING THEIR VILLAGE?

BECAUSE CAESAR MIGHT GET TO HEAR OF IT, AND I'M NONE TOO KEEN TO HAVE HIM ASKING ME WHAT I'M DOING HERE IN ARMORICA!

HALT! WE WILL PITCH CAMP HERE!

AND ONCE AGAIN WE ARE PRIVILEGED TO WATCH THE MANOEUVRES OF THE ROMAN ARMY. WHILE THE SAPPERS DIG A FOSSA (DITCH) AND RAISE AN AGGER (RAMPART)...

...THE WOODCUTTERS GO TO CHOP DOWN TREES...

...FOR THE CARPENTERS TO BUILD THE VALLUM (FENCE).

AT LAST THE CAMP IS READY. THE GENERAL AND HIS MEN ARE ABOUT TO ENTER IN REVIEW ORDER, THUS SYMBOLIZING THE MIGHT OF THE ROMAN ARMY, THE BEST-DISCIPLINED FIGHTING FORCE IN THE WORLD...

?

...ALTHOUGH SOMETIMES...

WHAT'S THAT?

MY TENT! I CAN'T STAND THE WAY THE OTHERS SNORE IN BED!

HERE'S ODORIFERUS, THE LEGIONARY I MENTIONED, O BRUTUS!

HOW DID YOU KNOW WE WERE LOOKING FOR A BABY, ODORIFERUS?

I SORT OF LIKE, HEARD THE PREFECT MENTION IT TO THE CENTURION AT AQUARIUM, O GENERAL, AND I LIKE, Y'KNOW NEARLY BROUGHT YOU THE BABY BACK!

SO WHAT STOPPED YOU?

HE DID! HE SORT OF TOOK ME FOR A RATTLE, Y'KNOW, AND THEN HE, LIKE, SWUNG ME AROUND OVER HIS HEAD, O GENERAL!

YOUR MAN SEEMS TO HAVE HAD A KNOCK ON THE CAPUT*!

BUT HE'S NOT QUITE KAPUT... AND HE MAY YET BE USEFUL!

*ROMAN HEAD.

WELL, IF THIS BABY LIKES PLAYING WITH RATTLES, YOU CAN TAKE HIM SOME, ODORIFERUS! DISGUISE YOURSELF AS A GAULISH PEDLAR AND INFILTRATE THE VILLAGE OF THE INDOMITABLE GAULS! THEN YOU CAN EASILY SNATCH THE BABY AND BRING HIM BACK TO US!

IF YOU AGREE, AND SUCCEED, YOU'LL GET TO BE OPTIO!

AND IF I, LIKE, SAY NO, Y'KNOW?

21 A

THEN YOU'LL, LIKE, GET TO BE DINNER FOR THE LIONS IN THE CIRCUS, **Y'KNOW!**

LATER...

DIDN'T YOU READ THE NOTICE? NO PEDLARS OR CIRCULARS IN THIS CAMP!

THE DISGUISE IS PERFECT... IT'S EVEN TAKEN IN THE SENTRY!

POC!

AND TO THINK I, LIKE, JOINED UP BECAUSE OF THE SMART UNIFORM!

LATER STILL, JUST OUTSIDE ASTERIX'S VILLAGE...

PAF!

GET OUT! NO PEDLARS OR CIRCULARS IN THIS VILLAGE!

21 B

?!

STOP HIM! STOP HIM! PROTECT ME!

ODORIFERUS, COME DOWN! AND THAT'S AN ORDER!

NO! NOOOO! I'D RATHER, LIKE, GO TO THE CIRCUS!

I HARDLY HAD TIME TO SPOT YOUR LITTLE FRIEND... BUT HE WAS AFTER THE PEDLAR, AND THE PEDLAR WAS IN SUCH A STATE HIS HAIR, BEARD AND MOUSTACHE HAD ALL DROPPED OUT!

! !

QUICK, OBELIX! WE MUST FIND THAT BABY!

DOGMATIX IS ALREADY ON HIS SCENT!

KEEP OUR BOARS ON ICE FOR US, FOTOGENIX. WE WON'T BE LONG!

SNIFF! SNIFF!

25A

THAT PEDLAR WAS NO MORE A GAUL THAN I'M A ROMAN! HE CAME TO KIDNAP THE BABY!

SNIFF! SNIFF!

IT'S A FUNNY THING, THE ROMANS BEING SO KEEN TO GET HOLD OF THAT CHILD!

YES! IT'S AS I ALWAYS THOUGHT.

WHAT IS?

THESE ROMANS ARE CRAZY!

TAP! TAP! TAP!

HERE HE IS, OBELIX! DOGMATIX HAS FOUND THE BABY!

DID YOU THINK HE WOULDN'T?

WOOF! WOOF!

HE'S FAST ASLEEP! WE MUSTN'T WAKE HIM!

I THINK HE'S DIGESTING THE PEDLAR!

FOR THE LAST TIME, ODORIFERUS, COME DOWN OR I'LL CHOP THE TENT POLE DOWN INSTEAD!

PROMISE ME THAT LITTLE MONSTER ISN'T IN THE CAMP!

I KNEW THAT MAN WAS UP THE POLE!

25B

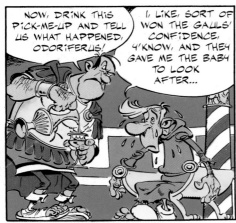

NOW, DRINK THIS PICK-ME-UP AND TELL US WHAT HAPPENED, ODORIFERUS!

I, LIKE, SORT OF WON THE GAULS' CONFIDENCE, Y'KNOW, AND THEY GAVE ME THE BABY TO LOOK AFTER...

I WAS GOING TO CARRY HIM OFF WHILE THEY WERE OUT, BUT THAT LITTLE MONSTER HAS, LIKE SUPERHUMAN STRENGTH, Y'KNOW, AND WHEN-EVER HE SEES ME HE SORT OF GOES INTO THE SAME ROUTINE, HE TAKES ME FOR A RATTLE AND...

HERE WE GO AGAIN!

EVEN THE GAULISH VILLAGERS ARE HAVING TROUBLE WITH HIM. ASTERIX HIMSELF ASKED IF I KNEW A NURSEMAID BRAVE AND STRONG ENOUGH TO LOOK AFTER HIM!

DID HE REALLY?

I THINK I'VE, LIKE EARNED PROMOTION TO OPTIO!

YOU? YOU'VE FAILED IN YOUR MISSION. THINK YOUR-SELF LUCKY NOT TO BE SERVED UP TO THE LIONS IN THE CIRCUS MAXIMUS!

I DIDN'T, LIKE, KNOW THESE PARTS BEFORE, BUT I WON'T BE SORT OF FORGETTING THE DIS-COVERY OF ARMORICA IN A HURRY!

WHAT HE SAID ABOUT THE NURSEMAID GAVE ME AN IDEA! WHY DON'T WE SEND ONE TO THE VILLAGE?

BECAUSE WE HAVEN'T GOT ANY NURSEMAIDS IN THE ARMY, THAT'S WHY!

PAF!

YES, WE HAVE... YOU!

WHAT DO YOU MEAN, ME?

THINK, CACTUS! THAT LUNATIC OF YOURS WAS WELL AND TRULY PUT THROUGH IT BY THE GAULS. WE MUST REMAIN THE ONLY ONES IN THE SECRET. AND IF YOU REALLY WANT THAT SEAT IN THE SENATE...

WELL, PROMISE ME NO ONE WILL GET TO KNOW, ANYWAY!

LATER...

AVE, GORGEOUS! LIKE A BIT OF SLAP AND TICKLE?

SLAP!

BY ZHUPITER! THAT'SH GOING A BIT TOO FAR!

IT WORKS! EVEN THE SENTRY WAS TAKEN IN!

(FALSETTO) MY NAME IS ASPIDISTRA, AND I HEARD YOU WERE LOOKING FOR A NURSE. I'M A VERY EXPERIENCED NURSEMAID!

?!

BUT YOU'RE NOT ONE OF OUR VILLAGERS... HOW DID YOU KNOW I WAS LOOKING FOR A NURSE?

(FALSETTO) OH, THESE THINGS GET AROUND THE LEGION... I MEAN THE REGION! SPECIALLY WHEN IT'S SOMETHING TO DO WITH THE BOLD AND FAMOUS WARRIOR ASTERIX!

!?

HOW ABOUT ME? DO THEY KNOW ABOUT **ME** IN THE REGION?

?

(FALSETTO) CAN I REALLY BE SPEAKING TO OBELIX, THE HANDSOME AND SEDUCTIVE MENHIR DELIVERY MAN?

HOWEVER DID YOU GUESS?

AND DID YOU ALSO HEAR THAT THE CHILD IN QUESTION IS... ER... RATHER A HANDFUL?

(FALSETTO) I'VE THUMPED... THAT'S TO SAY, I'VE BROUGHT UP WORSE, HANDFULS, I'M SURE!

28⁴

WE CAN ALWAYS TRY. GO ON, THEN, BUT DON'T SAY I DIDN'T WARN YOU!

FUNNY... I HAVE A FEELING I'VE SEEN HER FACE SOMEWHERE BEFORE!

MAYBE SHE'S NO MORE A NURSE THAN THAT MAN WAS A PEDLAR... WHAT DO YOU THINK OF HER, OBELIX?

A WOMAN OF TASTE AND DISCERNMENT!

WOMAN OF TASTE OR NOT, WE'D BETTER WATCH OUT!

TCHAC!

I DID WARN YOU! HE'S IMPOSSIBLE!

OH, I'M NOT RATTLED! I GOT OFF TO A FLYING START!

28⁵

I'LL GET THE BETTER OF YOU YET, YOU *@?&☆ CHILD!

CHLAC!

TEN TO ONE ON THE BABY!

YOU'RE ON!

IT'S NO USE TRYING TO TAME THAT LITTLE MONSTER, MY DEAR!

(NORMAL VOICE) MIND YOUR OWN BUSINESS!

I THINK THE NURSE'S VOICE IS BREAKING!

BUT I WAS ONLY GOING TO...

KEEP OUT OF THIS! GET BACK TO YOUR POTS AND PANS, WOMAN!

SPLATCH!

29a

FANCY SPEAKING TO THE CHIEF'S WIFE LIKE THAT!

YOU SEE, THE TROUBLE IS, THE BABY DRANK SOME MAGIC POTION LEFT AT THE BOTTOM OF A CAULDRON!

I'LL HAVE EARNED MY SEAT IN THE SENATE!

COME ON. I'LL TRY GETTING YOU OFF TO LESS OF A FLYING START!

LOOK! THE NICEST ASPIDISTRA IN THE WORLD! MUSTN'T HIT NICE ASPIDISTRA!

WAAH!

HERE WE GO AGAIN!

GOODBYE-EE, GOODBYE-EE, WIPE THE TEAR, BABY DEAR, FROM YOUR EYE-EE...

!

29B

UNDER THE LANTERNA, BY THE CASTRA* GATE... MY LILIUM OF THE LANTERNA LIGHT, MY OWN LILIUM MARLENA!

I DON'T THINK SHE'S MUCH BETTER THAN CACOFONIX!

BARBARIANS! YOU'RE ALL BARBARIANS!

LOOK, YOU CAN TELL THE BABY DOESN'T LIKE YOU MUCH!

*LATIN: BARRACKS.

A LITTLE LATER...

HE'S DROPPED OFF AGAIN! IT'S ALL RIGHT, YOU CAN LEAVE HIM TO ME NOW!

JUST ONE THING... HOW DO YOU COME TO KNOW THESE SOLDIERS' SONGS?

ER... A CHILDMINDER'S JOB DOESN'T PAY MUCH, SO I TOOK TO MINDING A ROMAN ARMY CANTEEN TOO. THERE ARE WAYS AND MEANS OF MOON-LIGHTING, AND THAT'S MINE...

...AND THAT WAY I GOT TO GE A MINE OF INFORMATION ON THE ARMY!

OH, WON'T I JUST HAVE EARNED MY SEAT IN THE SENATE!

WAAAH!

WELL, YOU'RE NEEDED AS A CHILDMINDER NOW!

31 A

OH, OH, OH, IT'S A LOVELY BELLUM...

COME ON, OBELIX! LET'S FIND SOMEWHERE QUIETER!

OH, GOOD WORK, VITALSTATISTIX! MARVELLOUS, I CALL IT!

WHAT? WHAT HAVE I GONE AND DONE NOW?

YOU'RE CHIEF OF THIS VILLAGE... YOU LET A WOMAN FROM OUTSIDE COME AND LIVE UNDER A BACHELOR'S ROOF? OH, THAT'S GREAT!

BUT PEDIMENTA DEAR, SHE'S ONLY A NURSE FOR THE BABY!

EXACTLY! SUCH PROMISCUITY! SHOCKING!

I'M NOT ENJOYING THIS ADVENTURE VERY MUCH, OBELIX!

OH, IT'LL BE ALL RIGHT! IT'S SURE TO END WITH A BANQUET UNDER THE STARRY SKY, SAME AS USUAL!

31 B

NEXT MORNING...

OH, I **WILL** HAVE EARNED THAT SEAT IN THE SENATE, AND NO MISTAKE!

BUT FOR THE EFFECTS OF THAT WRETCHED POTION, I'D TUCK HIM UNDER MY ARM AND MAKE OFF WITH HIM NOW!

BURP!

COME TO THINK OF IT, HOW DO I KNOW THE POTION'S STILL WORKING ON YOU, EH?

GA?

GA!

CLOCK!

EVERYTHING OKAY?

SORT OF... ARE THE EFFECTS OF THAT MAGIC POTION GOING TO LAST MUCH LONGER?

THAT DEPENDS! JUDGING BY OBELIX, THEY COULD LAST FOR EVER!

AND SO, A LITTLE LATER...

WELL, I'M NOT GOING TO STICK AROUND IN THIS ROTTEN VILLAGE FOR EVER, WEARING THESE ROTTEN CLOTHES AND PLAYING THIS ROTTEN PART!

TOO BAD! I'LL RISK IT!

WHERE ARE YOU GOING, GORGEOUS?

ER... I'M GOING INTO THE FOREST TO PICK MUSHROOMS!

?

WAAAH!

*LATIN: KIT-BAG.

SO THEY ARE... AND AT DAWN...

COCK-A...

COUGH-A... COUGH!

LOOK, ASTERIX! I'VE MET THE PEDLAR AGAIN!

AND I'VE MET THE NURSE!

IT'S A GOOD THING WE OUTNUMBER THEM, OR WE MIGHT HAVE BEEN MOVED!

NOW, TELL ME WHAT REALLY BROUGHT YOU HERE, OR YOU'LL HAVE A FEW TROUBLES OF YOUR OWN TO PACK UP IN YOUR OLD SARCINA!

MERCY! I WAS ONLY OBEYING THE ORDERS OF CAESAR'S SON, BRUTUS!

AND WHERE IS BRUTUS?

ON THE BEACH! HE KNEW YOU'D SEND THE BABY TO SAFETY THERE!

QUICK, OBELIX! FOLLOW ME!

QUICK, DOGMATIX! FOLLOW US!

WOOF! WOOF!

WHERE'S THE BABY?

ASTERIX, I HAVE FAILED YOU! A ROMAN SNATCHED HIM AND TOOK HIM ON BOARD A PIRATE SHIP!

I CAN STILL SEE IT ON THE HORIZON!

DO YOU THINK YOU COULD SWIM OUT THAT FAR?

YOU REALLY DO ASK STUPID QUESTIONS SOMETIMES, ASTERIX!

SORRY. I WAS ONLY THINKING...

WELL, OF COURSE I CAN!

I DON'T KNOW WHAT I'D DO WITHOUT YOU, OBELIX!

ALL SORTS OF SILLY THINGS!

SPLOSH! SPLOSH! SPLOSH! SPLO

SO WE'VE FIXED THE PRICE, THEN, ROMAN?

YES, BUT YOU DON'T GET PAID UNTIL WE DISEMBARK AT BRIVATES PORTUS*.

*BREST.

THAT'S OKAY! I'VE A WIFE IN EVERY PORTUS... SO THAT SUITS MY BRIVATE LIFE!

THE LAD MUST BE WORTH A LOT!

EVEN MORE THAN YOU THINK!

SHIVER ME TIMBERS... IF HE'S THAT VALUABLE, I'VE A GOOD MIND TO KEEP HIM FOR MYSELF!

TWO SWIMMERS ON OUR WAVELENGTH!

?

TWO SWIMMERS? WHO ARE THEY?

GAULS! THEY'RE MAKING WAVES! WE'RE IN DEEP WATER!

!

SURELY YOU'RE NOT ABANDONING SHIP JUST BECAUSE OF TWO GAULS?

YOU DON'T KNOW US, YOU NEVER SET EYES ON US, AND NOW WE'RE QUITS, ROMAN!

YOOHOO!

GOO!

COME ANY CLOSER, AND IT WILL BE THE WORSE FOR THIS BABY!

OUCH!

OW!

GRRRRR!

45

CLEOPATRA!

?!

AMAZING! WHAT A SIGHT!

AND WHAT A NOSE!

MY SON? CAESARION? BUT I THOUGHT YOU WERE BOTH SAFE IN MY PALACE IN ROME!

DID YOU SAY SAFE?

AFTER YOU LEFT, THE VILLAINOUS BRUTUS MADE SEVERAL ATTEMPTS TO DO AWAY WITH CAESARION, HOPING TO BECOME SOLE HEIR TO YOUR PROPERTY AND YOUR FORTUNE!

SO I DECIDED TO SEND OUR SON AWAY TO THE ONE PLACE WHERE I COULD BE SURE HE WOULD BE SAFE: THE VILLAGE OF INDOMITABLE GAULS WHICH STILL HOLDS OUT AGAINST THE INVADERS!

ALL RIGHT, I KNOW!

ET TU, BRUTE?* YOU WILL LEAVE IMMEDIATELY FOR UPPER GERMANIA! IT HAS A NICE BRACING CLIMATE, AND THE BARBARIANS THERE WILL TEACH YOU MANNERS!

*YOU TOO, BRUTUS? CAESAR SOMETIMES REPEATED HIMSELF.

FORGIVE ME FOR TAKING ADVANTAGE OF YOU, ASTERIX!

OH, THAT'S ALL RIGHT! I'M HONOURED BY YOUR FAITH IN ME, QUEEN CLEOPATRA!

THE... **THE BABY'S DISAPPEARED!**

THE END